THE MONEY SAVVY KID$™ CLUB

Home Sweet Home

Volume Three

By Susan Beacham & Lynnette Khalfani-Cox

Illustrations by Mary Jo Cadiz

Dedication

This book is dedicated to all families facing foreclosure,
and especially to children dealing with the loss of a home.

- Lynnette

Special Thanks

The authors wish to thank the following people for their brilliance and devotion

Illustrator: Mary Jo Cadiz

Editor: Cindy Richards

Poet: Michael Beacham

Money Savvy
GENERATION®
HELPING KIDS GET SMART ABOUT MONEY™

For award-winning tools to teach kids (ages 4-16) about money choices,
visit us on the web **www.msgen.com**

Publisher's Cataloging-In-Publication Da
Beacham, Susa
Home sweet home / by Susan Beacham & Lynnette Khalfani-Cox ; illustrations by Mary
Cadiz. SUMMARY: Four children learn about the responsibility of owning a house and t
impact on their families of not being able to pay a home mortgage loa
p. cm. – (The money savvy kids clu
ISBN 978-0-9842139-2
1. Money–Juvenile fiction. 2. Finance, personal–Juvenile fiction. I. Khalfani-Cox, Lynnet
II. Cadiz, Mary Jo (ill.). III. Title. IV. Seri
PZ7 .B3541 Ho 20(
813–dc.
LCCN# 2009935976
2nd editi

Isaiah, Dennis, Sandy and Stephanie were waiting for the morning bell to ring. It was Thursday, the day everyone would bring in a news story to discuss during Mrs. Berry's social studies class, when students would talk about current events.

The four friends had formed The Money Savvy Kids Club a year earlier. This year, they pledged to always bring in news stories about money. As they compared news clippings, Isaiah, Dennis and Sandy were surprised to see that each of them had chosen the same story to share today. The headline of the story read: "For Sale Signs Spring Up Around Town." The article talked about how lots of families were moving out of their town because they couldn't pay for their homes.

"I don't want us to talk about that," Stephanie said.

"Why?" Sandy asked. "Did you find a better article?"

"Well, no," Stephanie answered quietly, looking down at the ground. "It's just that I don't want to think about it because it's happening to my family. We're losing our house, which means I'll be losing my room. So will my little brother. Even my parents will lose their room. And I don't know what will happen to our cat."

Stephanie put her head in her hands and started crying. Her friends were stunned. Stephanie was always so tough. She never cried. Dennis was the first to speak up. "It's OK, Stephanie," he said, putting his arm around his friend.

Isaiah, who had been writing something in his notebook, looked up. "Yeah, Stephanie," he said. "I'm sure your parents will buy another house with a cool room for you. And I'll bet they'll stay right here in our neighborhood, so you won't even have to worry about going to a new school."

Stephanie looked doubtful. "My family is losing our house because it costs too much money," she explained. "Remember how I told you that my dad lost his job a few months ago?"

"Sure we remember," Isaiah said. "But I thought he got a new job."

"He did," Stephanie said. "But while he wasn't working, we couldn't pay all our bills. For awhile, my parents used our savings to keep up, but now our savings is gone too. Last night, my parents told us that we have to move out of our house. If we can't pay for this house, I don't see how we can afford to pay for a different one."

9

Just then, the bell rang and the friends headed off to class. When Mrs. Berry announced it was time for current events, Isaiah looked over at Stephanie. She nodded her head and said, "Yes, it's OK. We can talk about your news clipping." Immediately, Isaiah raised his hand.

"OK, Isaiah," Mrs. Berry said. "What news story about money do you have to share?" By now, Mrs. Berry knew she could count on The Money Savvy Kids Club members to bring in money news.

"Today, Dennis, Sandy and I all brought in the same article. It says there are a lot of homes for sale in our town. But we really don't understand why. The writer uses the words 'mortgage' and 'foreclosures' a lot and none of us really understands what those words mean."

Mrs. Berry smiled and said, "Well, Isaiah, you four children do give us new things to think and talk about. This is a very big story that has a lot of adults talking. But before we discuss mortgages and foreclosures as a class, I'd like you four to see if you can do a little research on your own. First you will need to find out what 'mortgage' means, then what it means when we say a home is in 'foreclosure.'"

"I guess we could go to the library after school and look up those words," Sandy said, thinking out loud.

"We can talk with Mr. Leaver, the librarian, and figure out our next step," Dennis added.

Isaiah, who had been taking some notes, looked up and said, "Yes, Mrs. Berry, we'll go to the library today and report back to the class tomorrow."

At the library, Mr. Leaver helped the members of The Money Savvy Kids Club go online so they could look up the words Mrs. Berry asked them to research.

Dennis started to sit down at the keyboard, but Stephanie stopped him. "Hey Dennis," she said. "Since this is happening to me, I think I'd like to be the one to do the research. Is that OK with you?" Dennis nodded and stepped aside as she sat down and started typing the word "mortgage" while Isaiah stood next to her, ready to take notes.

"It says here that a mortgage is a special type of loan that a 'lender,' like a bank, gives to people to buy a house. The lender charges a fee, or 'interest' on the money it lends to the people buying the home. Each month, people pay the lender some of the money they owe on the house plus some of the interest they owe," read Stephanie.

"Look up 'foreclosure' now," urged Isaiah.

"Well, it looks like they call people who get a loan from the lender to buy a house a 'borrower' and when the borrower can't pay back the loan money, their loan is foreclosed," Stephanie read as Isaiah continued to take notes. "That means the lender takes back the house and the people who lived there have to find somewhere else to live, just like me and my family," she said, looking as though she was going to start crying again.

"It's not just you," Sandy said. "The news clipping we brought into class said there are hundreds of families in our town that are losing their houses."

"But it doesn't say why so many people are losing their homes," said Dennis.

"I think I know," Sandy said. "My mom has told me about stuff like that." Mrs. Savingston, Sandy's mom, was an accountant who used to work for a bank so she was always a good source of information for The Money Savvy Kids Club. "She said that sometimes people borrow more money than they can afford or something happens so they can't pay their mortgage, like when Stephanie's dad lost his job or if somebody gets sick.

That's when they can lose their home because the lender will take the house and try to sell it. It's a way for the lender to get back the money it loaned for the house."

In a corner of the library, the friends organized their notes and the papers they had printed off the Internet. They were trying to decide what they would say in class. "We know the definition of mortgage and foreclosure, and we have an idea about why there are so many homes for sale. But we still don't know where Stephanie will live once her family moves," Dennis remarked.

"Let's get going," Isaiah suggested. "Maybe we can talk to Stephanie's parents to understand more about this."

When the gang arrived at Stephanie's house, they found her parents sitting together at the dining room table, looking at some papers. "Hi, kids," said Stephanie's mom. "How did things go at the library?"

They hadn't exactly planned on what to say to Stephanie's parents, so the four friends just stood there. Finally, Stephanie spoke up. "Mom, Dad, I know you said we have to move, and I don't want to add to your worries. But I am so sad that we have to leave the only house I've known my whole life, and I have a question," Stephanie said.

"What is it, honey?" her
father asked.

"Where will we live now
that we have to move?"
she asked.

26

"Well, your dad and I have a surprise for you," Stephanie's mom said as she picked up the papers they had been looking at. "We just signed a lease for the Johnsons' old house on Green Street. Remember how they had to move last year because Mr. Johnson's company moved to a new state? Well, they haven't been able to sell their house, so now they're renting it to us. It's good for us because we can afford it, and it's good for them because they'll be getting some money for a house they can't sell. And it's good for you because you'll still be able to go to your school, see your friends and be a member of The Money Savvy Kids Club."

Isaiah, who had been taking notes, looked up and smiled at Stephanie.

"So everything will be just like it was except I'll have a different room in a different house?" Stephanie asked excitedly. "And we can take our cat?"

"Of course we can take our cat," her dad said. "But everything won't be exactly like it was. We'll have a home, but we still have lots of bills we have to pay and we have to start building up our savings again. That all means we won't be able to spend as much on toys and eating out, and we'll skip our family vacation this year," he said as Isaiah took notes. Stephanie looked glum. Of all the members of The Money Savvy Kids Club, she was the one who most liked to spend her money.

"Come on, Steph," said Dennis. "It's not that bad. At least you'll all be together and you get to stay in the neighborhood."

"That's right," her father added. "And I just want you to know that your mother and I will always take care of you. We're your parents and we love you, so we'll always provide for what you need."

Isaiah, who had been writing furiously in his notebook, looked around at his friends and Stephanie's parents. He knew what they would say in class tomorrow: That change might be hard, but you can get through it, even if it's not something you were expecting.

The next day in class, when Mrs. Berry called on Isaiah to report back about mortgages and foreclosures, he told her that today Stephanie would be presenting the research for The Money Savvy Kids Club. Isaiah passed his notebook to Stephanie. Smiling once again, Stephanie walked to the front of the class and began to sing:

It's really quite funny,
This thing called money.

Houses cost a lot of money
And if you want to own
A bank may give you a mortgage
So you can make that house your home.

A mortgage is a home loan
A loan you must repay
Or the lender may foreclose on you
And you will have to move away.

The unexpected may occur
So you need to be prepared
With adequate savings to back you up
So that your bills can be squared.

A home is where your heart is
It's not a building but a place
A place you're warm and comfortable
That puts a smile upon your face.